Grandma's Magic Pillows

Based on a true story

Written by Karen M. Carlson
Illustrated by Laura Gilbert

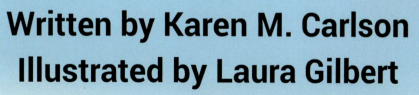

Once upon a time, there were three busy little brothers AJ, Jack, and Jase.

The boys were always busy playing something! Maybe building blocks, card games, or board games. When they weren't playing games, they were watching TV or running around playing tag and being a little crazy, like most little boys!

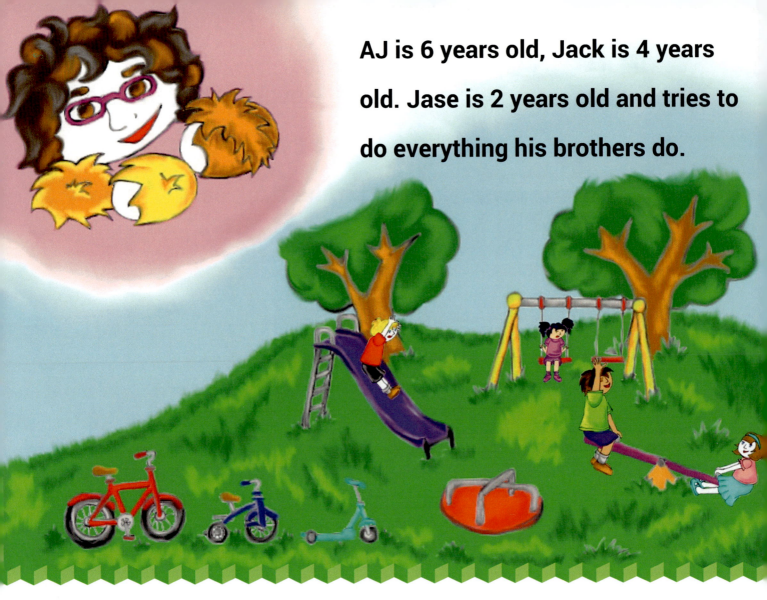

AJ is 6 years old, Jack is 4 years old. Jase is 2 years old and tries to do everything his brothers do.

Grandma Karen watches the boys while Mommy and Daddy work. They take trips to the three parks close by. When there are other kids at the park, they love playing together. They like to walk or take their bicycles, tricycles, and scooters.

They keep running and playing, or fighting over the same truck or toy.

They seem to stop only when sleeping or when they are in time out.

One day Grandma Karen brought some strange little pouches to the boys' house. "What are those?" AJ asked.

Jack excitedly asked,

Jase took one and just started throwing it.

"Are they for daddy's bean bag game?"

The boys were very curious. They did kind of look like the bean bags people use for bean bag toss games!

Grandma Karen explained, "It helps me calm down when I'm stressed."

Grandma Karen asked,

"Do you want to try it with me?"

This was something totally new. Grandma Karen said, "It's a game to see who can keep the eye pillow on the longest without it falling or slipping off."

It was hard at first to lie still so the Magic Pillow wouldn't slip off their eyes. Everything went black, which was very odd in the middle of a sunny day.

Grandma Karen set a timer on her phone for 2 minutes. They all lined up on the carpet. The boys were asked to be quiet, and they weren't even in trouble!

The boys started taking turns peeking out from under their eye pillow to see what was going on around them. Sometimes they were just itchy and twitchy waiting for the timer to chime.

Jack was giggly and wiggly. This made it hard for AJ and Jase to stay quiet. When Jack was noisy, Jase would put his fingers to his lips and say "Shhhhh."

AJ would ask,

"How much longer?"

When cousins Jackie and Becca were visiting, the floor was covered with children lying with Magic Pillows over their eyes. AJ told them, "We just lie down and be quiet. It's fun."

Grandma Karen left the eye pillows at the boys' house.

When Grandma said,

"Let's push the pause button,"

they knew exactly what that meant and ran to get their favorite Magic Pillow. It was quiet time. Each time it became easier. They learned to wait for the timer to chime.

Mommy's home!!

One week when the boys were having quiet time, Mommy came home before the timer went off. They all jumped up at once to see Mommy and give her hugs and kisses.

AJ went back downstairs and said to Grandma Karen,

"Can I do it again?"

Grandma Karen was really happy because now she knew they were enjoying their quiet time, and even asking for more.

Sometimes the boys would tell Grandma Karen, "I was thinking about . . . "

When the timer went off they would go back to playing and being busy little boys.

One day when Mommy was home, the boys were laying on the floor with their eye pillows. Mommy wondered what was happening. She thought,

"This isn't how my little boys usually act."

It was a big surprise! Mommy said, "These pillows are like magic." That's how the eye pillows got their name, Magic Pillows. Mommy now has her own Magic Pillow and loves it too.

How can this Magic Pillow quiet children? That is a good question. Grandma Karen knows it's good for children and adults to have some time just being quiet and calm during the day and now she could show them how.

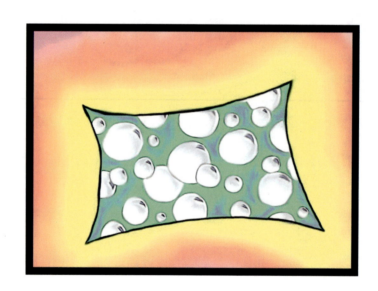

This is how the magic pillow came to AJ, Jack, and Jase's house. AJ asked Grandma Karen, "Can I show my friends?" It is very simple and easy to do. AJ, Jack, and Jase didn't think they would like it, but now they like it a lot!

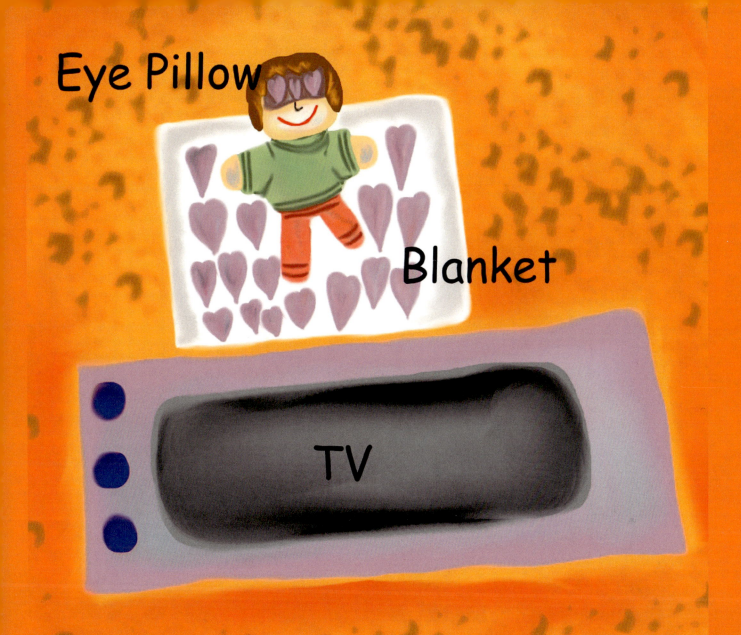

Illustration of AJ's Self-Portrait with Grandma's Magic Pillow

RELAXATION TIPS

Here are some practical ideas
for using the eye pillows with children.

- After getting ready for bed, brushing teeth, and storytime, use the eye pillow for a couple minutes. This will become a habit that cues children for sleepytime.
- Your child is ramping up to a major meltdown. What do you do? Use the eye pillow to diffuse the moment and slow your child down.
- Are you on a long car ride? Play some calm music and have them lay the eye pillow over their eyes. The time will fly by fuss-free.
- Is your child home from school and all wound up? Was it a stressful day? A couple minutes with their favorite eye pillow will change the energy instantly.
- Children's favorite activities and sports can drain their energy but they aren't sure how to slow down. Magic eye pillows to the rescue!
- Essential oils can be used for an additional benefit. Simple place a drop of oil on a tissue and lay it under the eye pillow so they can inhale it. You may also diffuse lavender or a calming oil in the room.

Additional eye pillows are available for adults and children

at Be Well And Renew online.

You can order them at www.BeWellAndRenew.com

Special orders are available upon request

for your child's favorite interest or superhero.

Contact Karen@BeWellAndRenew.com

630.542.7573

Enjoy this S.A.F.E. (Simple, Accessible, Fun, Effective) resource.

Calm and quiet children are possible!

WHAT KIDS SAY . . .

"The eye pillow helps me calm down when I get angry." ~ **Caleb, age 5**

"I can't wait to put my eye pillow on my eyes when I feel like everything is too much." ~ **Adam, Age 8**

"I like using my eye pillow at bedtime and sometimes after school when I just want to chill out." ~ **Susie, Age 7**

"I love the eye pillow. It helps me calm my anxiety and fears and helps me sleep better." ~ **Michael, age 9**

"I like the way my eye pillow smells and that it can just block out the world." ~ **Ronnie age 9**

WHAT ADULTS SAY . . .

"I put my Eye Pillow into my bag when I began a week of volunteering at a bereavement day camp for children and teens. I knew the 5 and 6 year olds would have lots of energy and limited attention spans. At the end of a long, first day, I brought out the eye pillow. Each child took a turn lying down in the center of our group's blanket. I set a timer on my phone for 90 seconds. No squirming, just rest. The others quietly watched as they waited for their turn. I've added this item and technique to my calming bag of tricks."
~ Lynne Staley, *Grief Educator and Life After Loss Coach*

"So many people of all ages struggle with stress and anxiety. I see patients younger and younger who are so overwhelmed and it affects their ability to function day to day. When I was introduced to these eye pillows I immediately began to refer them to a majority of my clients. They are such a beneficial tool that people can use to cope and decrease their anxiety. It's amazing how much they help!"
~ Samantha Bill, *LCPC, The Centered Life*

"As a migraine sufferer, I'm always look for tools to help blunt the pain. I never thought a little pillow would help! The lavender scented eye pillow has become my "Go To" option when I'm in pain and is incredibly effective. I am so thankful for these natural, effective tools."
~ Denise S. *C.O.O. ~ Women Entrepreneurs Secrets of Success*

DEDICATION

This book is dedicated to my grandchildren:
Ryan, Jenna, Jaclynn, AJ, Jack, Rebecca, Jase

Introducing the Magic Pillow to my grandchildren
began a wild and wonderful ride
that I never could have imagined.

The experience transformed my time with my grandchildren
and I found that it had a profoundly positive effect
on the lives of many other children as well.

I love each of you and am grateful for the abundant joy
you bring to my life.

<u>ACKNOWLEDGEMENTS</u>

I am eternally grateful that Laura Gilbert agreed to
illustrate this book.
It happened because I followed my belief and trusted
that she was the right person.
This took patience, but was completely worth it.
We had to wait for the timing to be perfect for both of us.
Her skill and inspired images brought this story to life
in a way that exceeded my hopes and dreams.

Thank You Laura!

About The Author

Karen Carlson has always been surrounded by children. It began by helping her mom with 4 younger brothers, then babysitting, then caring for her own three boys. Now Karen enjoys caring for grandchildren which brings great joy. Karen's love for caring translated into her wellness business, www.BeWellAndRenew.com which offers therapeutic massage and resources. Karen simply loves creating and caring. Karen now has published poetry, speaks on wellness topics, has recorded guided meditations, as well as the eye pillows to help adults and children enjoy quiet and calm in our busy world.

About The Illustrator

Laura Gilbert is a middle school language arts teacher and drama director. As you can imagine, her passions are reading, writing, and storytelling. However, an avid curiosity and a "How hard could it really be to do that?" -attitude has led her to explore and discover other talents. Cooking, gardening, painting - on canvas, on wood, on fabric, on stone, on glass - quilting, video design, scrapbooking, sewing doll clothes, and now, drawing illustrations.   Her husband and their two dogs are always supportive (with the dogs usually by sleeping on her feet as she works), no matter what new venture she wants to try.

29231068R00017

Made in the USA
Lexington, KY
29 January 2019